Livre de coloriage

Tous les animaux grands et petits

Young Scholar

All rights reserved. No part of this document may be reproduced
Used or transmitted in any form or by any means, electronic or otherwise. This means you cannot photocopy any material ideas or tips that are provided in this book.

Young Scholar
An imprint of Ciparum LLC

Livre de coloriage Tous les animaux grands et petits
© 2017 Ciparum LLC
All rights reserved.
ISBN-10:1-63589-241-4
ISBN-13:978-1-63589-241-3

www.youngscholar.co

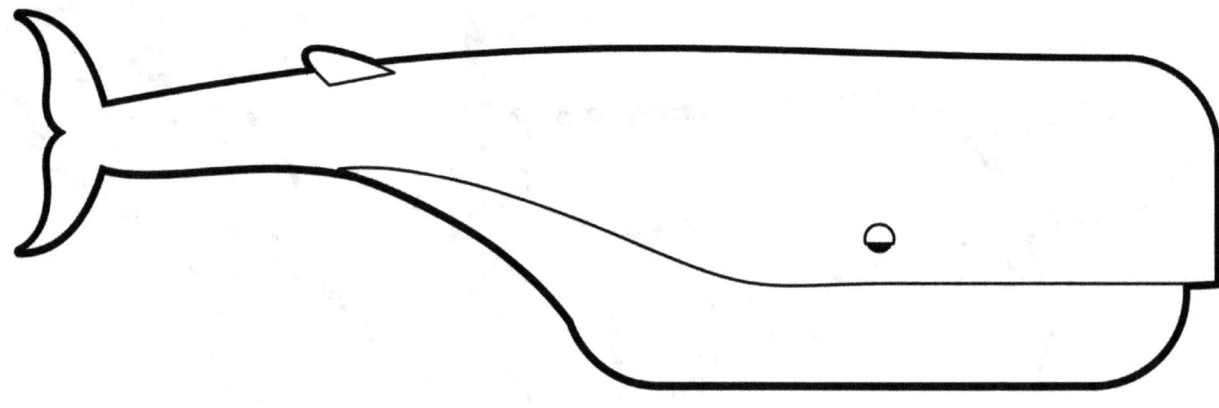

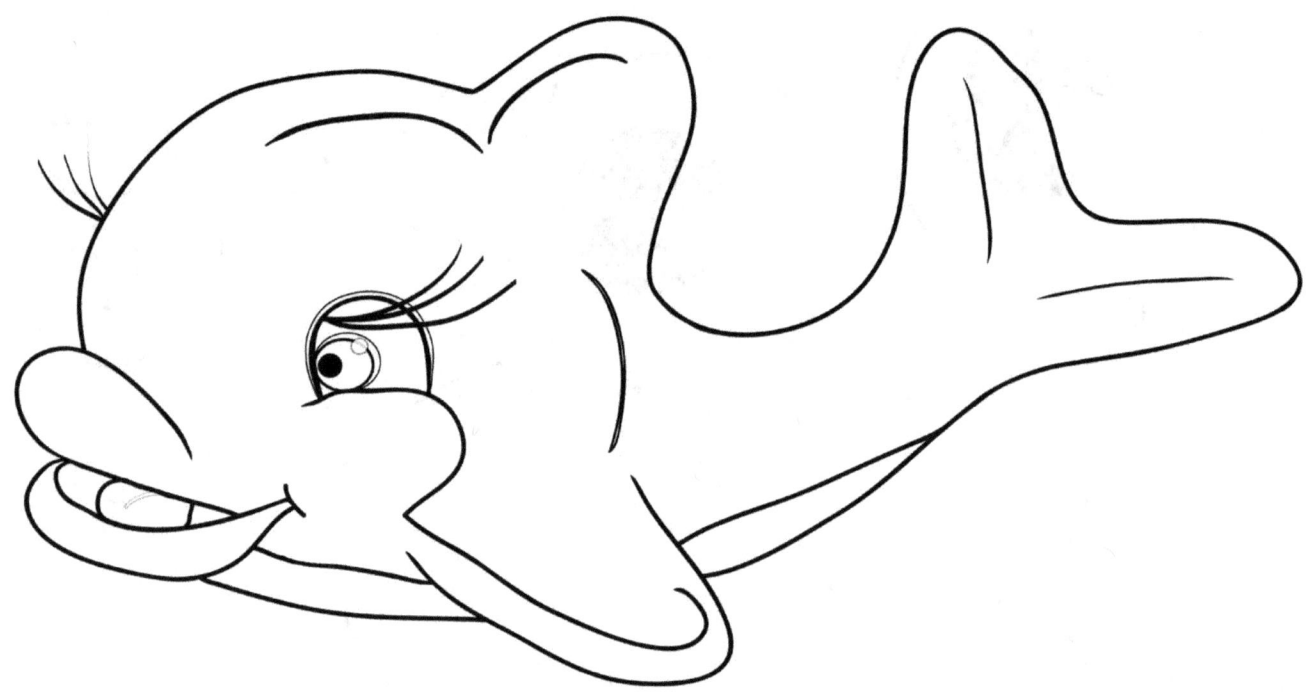